Ink of Tears

Echoes of Shattered Souls

Poetry Collections

Written By:

E.T. Mulloney

"Separation often carries a pain deeper than we can express, but there's a beautiful path to healing: **poetry**."

-E.T. Mulloney

Acknowledgments

I blame all of you, my exes.

In the intricate pattern of my life's journey, there's a

special thread woven by you, whose presence and

influence have left an indelible mark, drips of ink to my

core.

Through the highs and lows of our shared moments,

I found inspiration and a depth of emotion that gave birth to the poems within these pages.

Though our paths have taken different turns,

I carry with me gratitude for the part you played in shaping my poetic heartbreak journey.

These words are not just mine; they belong to us in the shared moments we once held

dear.

Your influence on my life and emotions has left a lasting imprint on these poems.

Thank you for being a part of my creative life's journey.

Contents

Ink of Tears

Echoes of Shattered Souls Poetry Collections

Introduction

In shadows cast, where
love did fall, A tale of
hearts, a crazy call.
Through tears and trials,
we shall explore, A
heartbreak's depths,
forevermore.

In these pages, a heart
shall break, A shattered
journey, for love's own
sake. In rhymes and
rhythms, emotions
collide, In this poetic
journey, our hearts
confide.

Within these verses, a
heart exposed,
A heartbreaking tale in words composed.
In ink and tears, emotions run,
A story of love, now all but done.

9

The Start.

In love's embrace, we

found our start,

But now we're worlds and miles apart.

Two shattered souls, we must depart,

In the echoes of our love, aching

hearts.

In love's grief,

we're torn apart, A

broken melody, a

shattered heart.

In love's agony,

we're torn in two,

Heartache lingers, a

pain so true.

In love's cruel grip, our hearts

did shatter, Promises

scattered, like dreams that

didn't matter.

Two wounded souls,

forever torn asunder, In

the abyss of hurt, we

both silently wonder.

.xxx.

Love's departure, my

heart in two, Lost

without you, what

can I do? Emotions

raw,

tears fall like rain,

In love's absence,

I'm filled with pain.

Missing Piece

In the quiet of night,

I ache for your grace,

Longing for your love,

in this empty space.

Your absence, a void,

my heart can't erase, In

the depths of longing,

I yearn for your embrace.

In the silence of our parting,

I'm deeply hurt, Longing

for your touch, my heart's

torn apart. Each moment

without you, like a jagged

shard, In this painful

longing, love's left deeply

scarred.

.xxx.

In bittersweet ink, our
love's tale I write, Desire to
touch you, understanding
sets it right.

In the ink of memories, our
love's song remains,
Burning desire to see you,
understanding restrains.

In the pages of my heart,
our love's story resides, A
burning desire to hold you,
understanding abides.

.XXX.

In the shadowed halls of grief,
I roam,
Lost in the echoes of a love once known.
A lover's absence, a pain hard to bear,
In this desolate abyss,
I find despair.

In the abyss of loss,

my heart does weep, A

lover's departure, my

sorrow runs deep.

Grief's heavy burden,

like a relentless cost, In

the haunting absence,

my love feels lost.

.XXX.

Love's agony, hearts torn

and scarred, In the void of

your absence, we're deeply

marred.

In the abyss of lost love, my

heart does ache, Each

memory a thorn, each step I

take. In your absence, my

world is forever changed,

Aching for your touch, our

love estranged.

Promises we made now haunt my dreams,

In the gallery of regrets, where

silence screams.

Lost in the ruins of what used to be,

I search for you, but you're not

here with me.

.xxx.

This pain, a river, deep

and unending,

In this love's tragedy,

I'm forever pretending.

That you'll return, and

this ache will cease, But

in this empty space,

there's no release.

In love's fading embers,

I'm left in the cold, A silent,

empty bed, where your

presence once told.

Each tear I shed is a letter unsent,

words of love and longing, to you,

I lament.

The echoes of your laughter,

still haunt these walls, In

the silence of our home,

your absence appalls.

Your scent lingers on, in

the clothes that you wore,

Reminding me of the love,

I'll feel nevermore.

.XXX.

The nights are the hardest, the

loneliness stings, In the

emptiness beside me, the pain

of your absence clings. Your

voice in my mind, a sweet,

fading song,

In the silence,

I long for where you belong.

Each morning I wake, to your
side, I reach out, But the space
beside me is empty, and filled
with doubt.

In love's cruel departure,
we both bear the cost,
Aching for the love, in
time, we have lost.

.XXX.

In your absence, my
world turns gray,
Lost in the echoes of love's decay.

The spaces you filled,
now empty and cold,
Memories of us, like
stories untold.

Your laughter, a ghost in
these silent halls, In the
emptiness, my heart often
falls.

Each morning,

I wake to your side, I

reach, but you're gone,

and your absence, still

preaches all day long.

In love's sweet pain,

I long for your embrace,

Each moment without you,

an endless chase.

The ache in my heart, a

reminder so clear, In the

symphony of longing, your

presence I revere.

Longing, like a dagger,

pierces my soul's core,

Lost without you, my

love, I implore.

In the void of your absence,

pain takes hold, Longing

for your touch, in the story

of love,

I'm told.

Each day without you,

a relentless strain, In

the sea of longing, my

heart feels the pain.

Lost in the echoes of our love's sweet refrain,

Longing for your presence, in my heart, the

hurt remains.

.XXX.

In the depth of my soul,

where memories reside,

Passionately longing, with

emotions to confide.

Bittersweet moments,

like stars in the night, I

yearn to relive them,

to hold you so tight.

.xxx.

Each memory's a treasure,

etched deep in my heart,

A canvas of love, a

timeless work of art.

In the garden of longing, our

moments do bloom, Aching

for their return, dispelling

the gloom.

Anger

In heart's wreckage,
anger's blaze does gleam,
Pain's ink spills, a poet's
wounded dream.

In the realm of shattered dreams,
I stand,
A poet of pain, with
anger in my hand.

Love's betrayal, a bitter,
searing brand, In these
verses of heartache, my
soul demands.

With ink of anguish, I
pen my plight, Each word
a dagger, cutting through
the night.

In the fire of anger,

my emotions ignite,

This broken heart, it

longs to take flight.

But as the ink flows,

and the pages fill, The

pain, the anger,

I'm determined to distill.

In this poetic lament,

I find my skill, To

heal my heart, and

reclaim my will.

.XXX.

In love's cruel game,

I was the pawn, Now a

poet of pain, in your

shadow I'm drawn.

In love's tender embrace,

I was led astray, Now a

poet of pain, in your

betrayal's dismay.

In your web of deceit,

I was ensnared, Now

a poet of pain, my

heart's laid bare.

Betrayed by your love,

a bitter, harsh sting, In

the verses of sorrow,

my emotions take wing.

.XXX.

In love's twisted tale,

I played the fool,

Now a poet of pain,

love's jest is cruel.

Deceived by your charms, my

heart's torn apart,

In the rhymes of betrayal,

I pour out my heart.

.XXX.

In love's anguish, our

worlds collide, Torn

hearts, lost dreams, on

this love we've died.

In your deceitful web, my

heart's frostbite, Goodbye

to your lies,

I'm taking flight.

A cold-hearted poet,

I'll no longer be your prize,

My heart's bleeding ink, as

our love finally dies.

Hopeful

In the depths of night,

my heart does ache,

A silent cry, a love's

bitter mistake.

Memories haunt, like

thorns they pierce, A

pain so deep, it's hard

to bear,

I fear.

But through this hurt,

I'll find my way,

To brighter skies,

a brand-new day.

.xxx.

In the garden of love,

we once did bloom, Two

souls entwined, under

the silver moon.

But as seasons changed,

so did our fate, Now

love lies shattered, at

Heaven's gate.

.XXX.

Your absence, a storm

that tears my sky,

In the abyss of longing,

I wonder why.

Promises whispered in the dead of night,

Now echo as ghosts, in the pale

moonlight.

Each word we shared, a

dagger's cruel thrust,

Leaving a trail of scars,

in love's cold dust.

A symphony of heartache,

a bitter refrain, In the

ruins of us,

I search in vain.

But still,

I hold fragments of our sweet past,

In the fragile hope, love may yet

outlast.

For broken hearts, though

wounded, can heal, And

love, once lost, in time,

may reveal.

.XXX.

So let us part, our paths

now diverge, In this

poignant chapter, we

must emerge.

For even in pain, there's
strength to find, In the
poetry of loss, our
hearts redefined.

.XXX.

In love's tender dance, we
found our grace, But now, it's
time for our separate space.

Two broken halves, once
whole, now apart, In the
gallery of memories, you'll
stay in my heart.

.XXX.

In the cavern of lovers' grief,
my heart does break, Each
teardrop shed, for love's
sake.

In the quiet night,

I mourn what's lost, A

symphony of heartache,

a tempest tossed.

Promises like fragile glass,

they shattered, In the void

of your absence,   my soul

tattered.

Lost in the labyrinth of love's cruel design,

I seek your warmth, but it's gone, and

you're not mine.

.*XXX.*

This heartbreak, a relentless,

cruel art, In the ruins of us,

where we once played our part.

Lovers' grief, a

painful,

unending song,

In this darkness,

I pray for love to prolong.

In love's cruel wake,

our hearts did rend,

Promises   broken,

our story's bitter end.

Yet from this pain,

we'll both emerge,

Stronger, wiser, our

hearts will surge.

.XXX.

In love's cruel grasp, we're

torn and scarred, Yet in

the aching void, hope's

flame still marred.

Though hearts are broken,
they can still mend, In
love's ruins, a chance to
transcend.

.XXX.

In love's shadow, we
both are torn, But hope
endures, though hearts
are worn.

From this ache, new
strength will rise, In
love's demise, our
spirit flies.

.XXX.

In the vault of memories, pain
resides,
Each moment cherished, now
a wound that abides.

Love's echoes haunt, in
every thought they play,
In the tapestry of hurt, we
find our way.

.xxx.

In the depths of my being,
where emotions reside, A
passionate longing, for
moments by your side.

Bittersweet memories,
like pages in a book, I
yearn to revisit them,
to take another look.

.xxx.

Each memory's a treasure,
in the archives of my soul,
A masterpiece of love, a
story to make me whole.

In the symphony of longing,

your presence I trace, Hoping to

relive those moments, in your

warm embrace.

.xxx.

In the canvas of love, where

our story once bloomed, I'm

now a poet of pain, my heart

deeply consumed.

Betrayed by your actions,

in this cold, bitter night, I'm

haunted by shadows, lost

in love's blight.

.XXX.

Deception's cruel dance, in
your eyes I discerned, As
our love's bright flame, in
your lies, was burned.

In the echoes of your deceit,
my heart aches and mourns,
A lover betrayed, in the
thorns of love,
I am torn.

.XXX.

Sadness

In love's bittersweet embrace,
we once thrived, Now, in
silent solitude, we've both
dived.

Promises like petals fell,
one by one, In the ashes
of us, our love undone.

.xxx.

In love's cruel game, we
both were players, But
now, we're just two,
broken-hearted betrayers.

Words once sweet, now cut
like sharpened knives,

In this shattered love, we've
ruined our lives.

.XXX.

In love's wreckage, we
stand torn asunder,
Our once-tender bond,
now shattered asunder.

Promises   broken,
hearts left in debris,
In this desolate love,
we're no longer "we."

.XXX.

In love's cruel storm,
we   both   drown,
Broken hearts,
tears fall,
we're forever down.

Love's departure, a
cruel twist of fate,
Left in its wake,
emotions I can't abate.

Heartache's grip, like
a vice so tight, In the
shadows of us,
I search for light.

Each memory, a dagger
in my heart, In the
canvas of our love, a
tearful art.

Emotions raw, like a
thunderous rain,
In the abyss of loss,
I bear the pain.

.xxx.

In love's passionate storm,

we were swept away,

Emotions ran high, in

tumultuous disarray.

But as the tempest subsides,

we're left in the rain, Aching

hearts, in this sea of emotions

and pain.

In love's tempest, our

hearts took flight, But

in its aftermath, we

both feel the bite.

Emotions like lightning,

they struck us so deep, In

the storm's aftermath,

our love weeps.

.XXX.

In love's tempest, we

ventured so bold,

Leaving us with scars,

stories untold.

The weight of those memories,

heavy and grim, In the

aftermath, our love's chances,

seem slim.

.XXX.

In the deep well of longing,

a piercing pain, For your

touch, your love,

I ache in vain.

Lost in the abyss of your absence,

I remain,
In the shadows of our love,

there's only rain.

.XXX.

With tears in my eyes,

I yearn to the past,

Bittersweet memories, too

beautiful to last.

I long for those moments,

a love unsurpassed, In

the hope they'll return,

my heart holds them fast.

With tears in my eyes,

and a heart that's torn,

Bittersweet memories,

like roses with thorns.

I ache for those moments, now

distant and few, Longing for

their return, to rekindle love

anew.

.xxx.

Tears in my eyes, bittersweet
memories unfold, Longing
for the past, a love story
untold.

In the shadows of time,
where our hearts had been, I
ache for those moments, to
live them again.

In the depth of my pain,
a silent cry, Sorrow's
heavy burden,
I can't deny.

But in this darkness, a
glimmer I see,

A resilient heart, seeking
to be free.

.XXX.

In the labyrinth of love,
I once found my way, A
hopeless romantic, in
the light of your day.

But now, in shadows,
my heart is betrayed, By
a lover's deception, in
your web I'm enslaved.

Your words, once sweet,
like a melody divine, Now
taste like bitter poison, in
this heart of mine.

.XXX.
The promises we made,

like castles in the air,

Now crumble to dust, in

the wake of your affair.

I gave you my trust, my

soul, and my heart, But

you played a game,

tore our love apart.

In the wreckage of us,

I'm left to mourn, A

hopeless romantic,

in love's bitter thorn.

Yet, in my pain, a flicker

of hope remains, That

someday, love's wounds,

will mend their chains.

But for now,

I'm a poet of sorrow and despair,

A hopeless romantic, betrayed

and left in the snare.

In the depths of my being,

memories sharply sting,

Great moments we had,

now an ache they bring.

.xxx.

Regrets, like a storm, in

my heart they unfold, In

this bittersweet farewell,

love's story grows cold.

Regrets

In the silent night,
"what if" softly weaves,
Aching with passion, for
what we could achieve.

Tears whisper regrets, in
the darkness they sigh,
In the "what if" of love,
our hearts still try.

In the tearful night,
I ponder what might be,
Aching with "what if," in
this love's decree.

Passion once burning,
now smoldering, ember's
glow, In the realm of
longing, my heart's
bittersweet woe.

45

What if, we'd chosen a different path to
take, Could we, have avoided this heart-
wrenching ache?

In the depths of my soul,
a question does persist, In
the poetry of "what if,"
I seek solace and twist.

But in the end, we walk the
path we must, Though "what
if" may haunt,
in faith I'll trust.

.xxx.

For life's twists and turns,
they shape our story's blend,
In the tapestry of tears, love's
lessons we'll transcend.

In the hush of night,

"what if" softly sighs,

Aching for moments lost, in

the starlit skies.

Tears trace the paths of dreams,

that might have been, In the

"what if" of love, our hearts

remain keen.

In the still of night,

"what if" does linger,

Aching with passion, love's

missed out bringer.

Tears in my eyes, they

softly confess, In the

realm of "what if,"

love's bittersweet caress.

As the night embraces,

"what if" takes its flight,

Aching and hopeful, in

the fading moonlight.

Tears find their rest, as

the dawn draws near,

In the "what if" of love,

we release our fear.

.XXX.

In the realm of shadows,

my heart weeps and sighs,

A tragic loss, where love

forever lies.

Your memory, a star, in my

night's darkened skies, A

love that once soared, now

aching goodbyes.

.XXX.

"I love you still, but if only,"

I whisper, in pain,

Great moments we shared,

I long to rewind again.

Regrets, like a shadow, in

my heart they instill, In

this bittersweet farewell,

love's echo lingers still.

"I love you still, but if only,"

my heart cries, Great

moments we shared, now

masked by goodbyes.

Regrets, like a torrent,

through my soul they spill,

In this bittersweet farewell,

love's ache is a bitter pill.

"I love you still, but if only,"

I cry to the night,

Great moments we cherished, now

fading from sight.

"I love you still, but if only,"

my heart breaks the spell,

Great moments we shared,

in my soul, they dwell.

Regrets, like relentless

waves, my emotions they

steal, In this bittersweet

farewell, love's wounds,

time won't heal.

"I love you still, but if only,"

my heart aches to say,

Great moments we had, in

my mind, they replay.

Regrets, like a shadow,

upon my heart they rest, In

this bittersweet farewell,

I hope you'll find your best.

Healing

In love's wreckage, we
stand torn apart,
Promises shattered,
aching hearts.

In the ruins of us,
we find our way,
Healing   slowly,
day by day.

.xxx.

In love's bitter wake,
revenge may brew, But
remember,
it taints the heart it's true.

Let's heal, not harm, as
we part ways, In
kindness and growth,
brighter days.

.XXX.

In love's fiery blaze, we dared
to ignite, Passion's flames
burned bright, yet not quite
right.

In the embers of pain, we
must now ascend, From
the fire we stoked, find a
love to mend.

.XXX.

In the caverns of my heart,
sorrow dwells, A silent
ache, a tale it tells.

But in this darkness, hope
persists,
In my brokenness,
I'll find what exists.

.XXX.

In the echoes of loss,

anger takes hold, Ghostly

reveries of love, now

bitter and cold.

A fire once burning,

now ashes remain, In

the depths of my rage,

I seek to reclaim.

But, as I navigate this

tempestuous sea, I'm haunted, by

memories of you and me.

In this storm of anger,

I'll find my way through, To

a place of acceptance,

where healing is true.

New Beginning

In love's painful rift,
we found our fate,
Promises shattered,
hearts left to ache.

But from the wreckage,
we'll each reclaim, New
beginnings arise, from
love's fiery flame.

.XXX.

In love's shattered realm,
we find our verse, A
painful tale, where
hearts rehearse.

Once intertwined,
now torn asunder, A
symphony of pain,
like distant thunder.

.XXX.

In your absence, my world
has lost its glow, In every
shadow, your presence
seems to flow.

Promises   whispered,
now echo as regrets, In
the ruins of our love,
my heart resets.

Each memory a thorn, a
relentless sting, In the
gallery of what was, my
soul takes wing.

.XXX.

Lost in the labyrinth,
of love's cruel design, I
search for solace, but
it's nowhere to find.

This heartache, an endless,
mournful song, In the
script of lost love, where
we both belong.

.XXX.

With pen in hand,
I write our bittersweet rhyme,
In the annals of heartbreak,
for now, it's our time.

But though we're broken,
we'll rise above, For in
the ruins of love, we'll
find self-love.

.xxx.

Our story may end, but
our spirits will soar, In
the poetry of healing,
we'll be hurt no more.

.xxx.

In the depths of my soul,
the echoes persist, A
forever broken heart, in
the abyss I exist.

But with pen in hand,
I'll close the chapter,
so bold, Write a new
story, in the ink of
my soul, but not old.

Closing

Bittersweet memories, like
thorns in the heart, Love's
once vibrant canvas, now
torn apart.

In the album of memories,
joy and tears, Our love's
bittersweet, echoes
through the years.

.xxx.

In love's tender dance, we
found our grace, But now, it's
time for our separate space.

Two broken halves, once
whole, now apart, In the
gallery of memories, you'll
stay in my heart.

.XXX.

In the symphony of heartaches,
our love did wane, A once-
vibrant melody, now met with
pain.

Two hearts now heavy,
aching and sore, In the
echoes of heartaches, we
part forevermore.

.XXX.

In love's fiery furnace,
we were once consumed,
Passion's inferno, our
desires unbridled, and
assumed.

But in the scorching blaze,
we both got burned, Fire

and pain, a lesson we had

to learn.

.XXX.

The flames of attraction,

they danced so high, In

their searing glow, we

dared to defy.

But as the fire raged,

it left scars behind, In

the agony of love, we

had to realign.

The heat of your touch,

a burning sensation, Yet

beneath the surface, a

gnawing frustration.

Our love, like wildfire,

it raged and roared,

But in its wake, our

hearts were left,

scarred and sore.

.XXX.

Now, as the embers fade,

and the pain takes its toll, We

must rebuild our hearts, heal

our wounded soul.

For in the midst of the fire,

we found our strength, In

the poetry of pain, a love

of greater length.

.XXX.

So, let us not be consumed,

by the flames that remain,

But rise from the ashes, and

love again.

.XXX.

In the midst of this love turmoil,

my dear, A humorous, sexy side

begins to appear.

Despite the hurt, a

twinkle in my eye, For

your passionate touch,

oh, how time does fly.

Our playful banter, once

a secret delight, Now

tinged with longing, it

ignites the night.

In this hurtful passion, we

find a hidden thrill,

Yearning for your touch,

can't get my fill.

In this comical chaos,

of love's grand scheme,

A sexy, humorous

twist, like in a dream.

.XXX.

Though hurting, there's a playful

spark in our dance, Yearning for

your touch, a tantalizing chance.

Our laughter, once

shared, now a

bittersweet potion, In

this hurting passion, a

curious emotion.

Through the pain, a

flirtatious desire,

does gleam,

Yearning for your

love, like an elusive

dream.

In this love's absurd comedy, so

sly,

A sexy humor, as

we say goodbye.

Though hurting hearts, we

share a knowing glance,

Yearning for your touch,

in this wild romance.

.xxx.

Our jokes, once innocent,

now tinged with heat, In

this hurting passion, our

hearts still beat.

Through the tears, a
playful fire does burn,
Yearning for your love,
it's your touch I yearn.

In love's cruel theater, the
final act nears, Aching,
longing, drowning in our
tears.

The humor we shared,
now lost in the night,
Yearning for your touch,
I fade from your sight.

Our playful banter, once
a refuge from pain, Now
echoes in silence, a loss
hard to explain.

.XXX.

As we close this chapter, in
a story we both host, The
hurtful longing remains, a
love now lost.

.XXX.

In love's intricate maze, we
wandered astray, Aching
hearts, in the dance of our
own ballet.

Though hurt and longing,
our paths may differ, In
the tapestry of love,
we're both left to wither.

Our memories, once vivid,
now shrouded in mist, In
the labyrinth of time,
they persist.

As we part ways, with a
heavy heart, I must, bid
farewell, to what once
was, and embrace what
is just.

.XXX.

In the passionate tango, of
our love's last stand, Grief
and sorrow entwined,
hand in hand.

With longing hearts, we
waltz into the night, The
bittersweet embrace,
our final sight.

The memories we cherished,
a fire that burned, Now
smoldering embers, in
silence, we've learned.

As we part ways, in this
passionate goodbye, The
tears of our love, like a
river, they'll dry.

In the mournful night,
love's lost forevermore,
Aching in my heart, an
ache I can't ignore.

.XXX.

Tears fall like rain, in the
shadows I grieve, In the
silence of lost love,
I can't believe.

In the mournful night,
love's ghost does haunt,
Aching for a touch, a
love we'll never flaunt.

69

.xxx.

Tears blend with rain, as
our story's end nears, In
the abyss of lost love, my
heart drowns in tears.

In the silent night, love's
flame is extinguished,
Aching for what's gone, our
hearts relinquished.

Tears fall as we part,
love's cost we now sever,
In this mournful ache, we
say goodbye forever.

.xxx.

In the silent void, my heart's
lament does start, A tragic
loss, a love torn apart.

Your absence, a wound, forever
etched in my core, A love once
vibrant, now lives in memories
evermore.

.XXX.

In the ruins of my heart,
a poet I stand, Forever
broken, in a desolate
land.

With trembling hand,
I close the chapter's toll,
To write anew, with
echoes of my soul.

.XXX.

In the chambers of despair,
my heart does reside, A
forever broken poet,
where emotions collide.

With tear-stained pages,
I close the chapter's toll, To
write anew, releasing
echoes of my soul.

.XXX.

In the abyss of torment, my
pen finds its place,
Forever broken,
I'll etch my disgrace.

With each painful stroke, my
soul's anguish I'll show,
Closing the chapter, in my
heart's wretched throes.

In the bittersweet symphony,

of memories past, I bid

farewell, our love's die cast.

.XXX.

Great moments,

like jewels, in my heart

they'll remain, Closing this

chapter, with love's

enduring refrain.

In the shadows of your lies,

my heart does freeze, A

lover's deceit, like a

chilling breeze.

You wounded me deeply,

with your callous art, So

now, in icy verses,

I'll depart.
Your promises were empty,

like a vacant sky, I'm

.XXX.

leaving behind this love,

this cruel lie.

In the coldness of your actions,

I find my reply, A

cold-hearted   poet,

bidding love goodbye.

.XXX.

In the ruins of our love,

my heart's now frayed,

Feelings for you, in

darkness,

I've laid.

Farewell to your deceit,

my emotions are shy, A

cold-hearted poet, love's

flame has gone dry.

In the frosty echoes of our love's sad song,

I'll find strength and purpose, and carry

on strong.

No longer ensnared, in

your deceit's bitter snare,

As a poet reborn,

I'll find beauty in the air.

So farewell to the lies, the

heartache, the pain, In

the verses of my future, a

new love will reign.

A cold-hearted poet, now
set free to fly, Bidding
farewell to the past, under
a hopeful sky.

In your treacherous wake, my
heart's become cold, Feelings
for you buried, forever
untold.

Farewell to your deception,
in my ink, I comply, A
cold-hearted poet, it's
time to say goodbye.

Understanding

In the depths of grief, our
hearts entwine, Love's pain
echoes, a constant,
haunting chime.

Amidst the anguish, we
both endure, Love's
sorrowful burden, we
must mature.

.XXX.

In the garden of love, we
once did bloom, Two
hearts entwined, under
the crescent moon.

But as seasons changed,
so did our fate, Now
love lies shattered, at
Heaven's gate.

.xxx.

Your absence, a storm

that tears my sky,

In the abyss of longing,

I wonder why.

.xxx.

Promises, whispered in the

dead of night, Now echo as

ghosts, in the pale moonlight.

Each word we shared, a

dagger's cruel thrust,

Leaving a trail of scars,

in love's cold dust.

.xxx.

A symphony of heartache,

a bitter refrain, In the

ruins of us,

I search in vain.

But still,

I hold fragments of our sweet past,

In the fragile hope, love may yet

outlast.

.xxx.

For broken hearts, though

wounded, can heal, And

love, once lost, in time,

may reveal.

.xxx.

So let us part, our

paths now diverge,

In this poignant chapter, we
must emerge.

For even in pain, there's
strength to find, In the
poetry of loss, our
hearts redefined.

.XXX.

In love's fiery embrace,
we danced with desire,
Our hearts aflame, a
tempest of passion,
higher and higher.

But in the depths of lust,
we lost our way, In the
aftermath, our love's
price we'd pay.

The heat of passion, a
wildfire untamed, In
the flames of longing,
we both were maimed.

But as the embers faded,
reality came near, Lust
turned to pain, as we faced
our deepest fear.

The touch of your skin,
a burning sensation,
But underneath it all, a
haunting realization.

Our love, like wildfire,
consumed and left bare, In
the smoldering ruins, all
we had was despair.

Now, in the aftermath of our feverish
affair, Lust and pain intermingled, a
heavy cross to bear.

Two souls, once entwined in a
passionate dance, Now wounded and
scarred, left with one last chance.

.XXX.

To heal the wounds, to
find a love that's true,
In the ashes of lust,
we'll start anew.

For while passion burned bright,
it also left pain, In the poetry of
our love, we'll find peace again.

In the shadowed chambers of my soul,

I weep, A symphony of

sorrow, my secrets I

keep.

The weight of heartache,

like a burden I bear, In

this tale of sorrow,

I find solace in despair.

.*xxx.*

Through the labyrinth of pain,

my spirit does roam, In

search of healing, a place to

call home.

.*xxx.*

Each tear that falls, a

verse in my rhyme,

In the poetry of grief,

I'll find strength in time.

.*xxx.*

For though the night is long,

and the road is steep,

Hope's ember flickers, in

my heart, it'll keep.

In the echoes of pain, there's

a flicker of light,

In this brokenness,

I'll find my way to the light.

.XXX.

With every sunrise, a

chance to renew, In the

tapestry of sorrow, my

colors will be true.

For life's deepest wounds,

they often impart, The

wisdom to heal, and

mend a broken heart.

.XXX.

So, I'll write my story, in

ink and in tears, In the

chronicles of pain,

I'll conquer my fears.

.XXX.

From the ashes of sorrow, a

phoenix will rise,

With a hopeful heart,

I'll embrace new skies.

In the chambers of my heart, a

bittersweet melody plays, As I

bid farewell to our memories,

in love's gentle blaze.

.xxx.

Great moments, like stars,
forever they'll gleam, In
the tapestry of our love, a
cherished, fading dream.

With each whispered goodbye,
a part of me you take, In the
echoes of our laughter, the
love we used to make.

Great stories, like old books,
on the shelf, they'll rest, In
this bittersweet farewell,
our love's final test.

.xxx.

Though we part ways now,

our souls forever twined,

In the depths of my heart,

your memory I'll find.

.xxx.

Great love, like a sunset, fades

with the night, But in the dawn of

new beginnings, we'll find our

light.

Conclusion

As we reach the end, of

this heartrending story,

In the fading echoes, of

love's fleeting glory.

Let us remember, the tears

and the pain, For in

heartbreak's embrace, we

rise again.

.XXX.

As we close this chapter,

hearts embrace, In

sorrow's wake, we

found our grace.

Through tears and trials,
love's legacy lives, In
bittersweet memories,
our hearts forgive.

.*xxx*.

In the final pages, of
this tear-stained book, A
bittersweet ending, a
somber, heartfelt look.

Through love's trials, and the
tears that fell like rain, In this
closing chapter, we find
strength in pain again.

.*xxx*.